COPING STRATEGIES

SELF DETECTIVE

Published in 2020 by FeedARead.com Publishing

Copyright © Self Detective

First Edition

A CIP catalogue record for this title is available from the British
Library.

PART 1.

Introduction to coping strategies

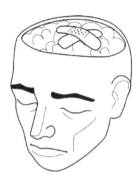

It seems important to say straight away that coping strategies do not resolve the causes of our distress. Instead, they exist to reduce our levels of stress so that we can continue to function.

For some people this will be fine, since coping is the very best they can hope for. (For some people coping could be seen as an Olympic gold medal – an impressive feat of courage and endurance.)

For others, coping only makes matters worse, and what they actually need is time in recovery – away from their day-to-day life. This can be a hard thing to admit, especially if they have high expectations of themselves.

There are also people who use coping strategies as a springboard to wellness, to get themselves into a routine where they then feel able to move forward and improve the quality of their lives.

Finally, there are those who have had a temporary dip in their fortunes and may only need to cope for a short amount of time – to avoid things escalating and becoming worse.

Whichever stage you may be in your life, we hope that this section gives you some insights into the wider world of coping.

PART 2.

Stress

In 1936, Hans Selye designed a **3-stage model** to help explain the process of stress and how we respond to it. From his research, he found that the body places huge importance on maintaining a healthy balance at all time. If there is an imbalance, the body seeks to redress this as quickly as possible by releasing hormones into the system, in the hope that the stress can be overcome in a matter of minutes.

Stage one is the **alarm** stage, where an alert is sent around the body to prepare for a threat. The resulting emergency reaction is often called the flight or fight response, as adrenaline and cortisol are produced to give you greater strength, energy and heightened awareness.

Stage two is about **resistance**. The body is now as ready as it will ever be to resist the stress, but it cannot do so for long before it weakens.

If the stress continues for some time, the third and final stage is likely to be **exhaustion**. Here the body cannot resist the stress any longer. Ideally at this stage, the body is looking to repair itself as soon as it can. If this is not an option, the body is in danger of facing burnout.

Signs of burnout

Just because you are coping doesn't mean you are necessarily okay.

Burnout is the effect of being immersed in stress for a long time. Burnout can be revealed through bodily sensations, feelings, actions or thought processes. Here are some examples:

- being consistently less productive and less able to sleep
- becoming more irritable, apathetic, detached from the world
- getting overwhelmed with feelings of hopelessness and despair
- becoming more tired and drained and lacking in energy
- increased susceptibility to illness
- becoming forgetful, angry, depressed and anxious
- being less enjoyable for others to be around

To recover from the effects of burnout, please read on and look for coping strategies that work best for you.

Richard Lazarus had another way of looking at stress, using a **2-stage approach** that he developed in 1984. He saw the process of stress and our response to it as dependent on: (i) the type of person we are (ii) how we size up the stress we face (iii) the environment we are in when we are stressed, and (iv) the coping methods that are available to us at that moment in time, be they our own internal methods of coping or anything external that may help or hinder us (like another person, say).

Exams, operations, separations, public speaking, new jobs. According to Lazarus none of these needs necessarily be stressful as a matter of course. We *make* them stressful, by loading them with our own hopes, fears and worries. We *make* them stressful by defining them as stressful.

In his model, it is the perception of stress that is of more interest than the actual stress itself.

If we think something is stressful, it will become stressful. If we don't, it may not. For some people, say, there is a fine line between excitement and anxiety. A person could be excited but define it (or misinterpret it) as anxiety – or vice versa.

Lazarus splits up our perception of stress into two stages:

The **primary appraisal stage** is all about deciding if an event or a situation is stressful or not, or whether it is insignificant, or perhaps of benefit, or possibly mildly annoying, etc.

If it's deemed to be stressful, in what way is it stressful?

Harm   Loss

Threat   Challenge

Here you may be asking questions based on something that has already happened. For example: how dangerous is the **harm** of the illness/injury? How much blood has been **lost** already? Or you may be sizing up a potential **threat** to your well-being, such as walking down a dark street at night. Or you may be working out what you have in your own locker (or, say, your own toolkit) to overcome a potential **challenge**.

The **secondary appraisal stage** follows on from the first stage. Here a notion is formed as to how well you are going to cope with the stress from the harm-loss-threat-challenge. If you are confident you can cope, your stress will go down. If you are not so sure, your stress levels might go up.

Acknowledging the need to find a coping strategy is a recognition that we do not have enough resources available to manage the stress.

Needing to find a coping strategy puts us into two possible camps:

Problem-focused coping	Emotion-focused coping

Problem-focused coping looks at ways to solve the issues that are causing and creating the stress. This could involve some sort of planning or changing the way you do something.

Emotion-focused coping looks at ways to manage the emotional response of the stress. This could involve avoiding certain situations, or it could be to actively engage in something.

Active coping	Avoidance coping

For example, consciously spending more or less time with your family members.

Finally, another way of dividing up your coping options is to look at whether or not you have a positive or negative outlook on the matter at hand.

Positive outlook	Negative outlook

For example, one definition of anxiety is overestimating danger and underestimating your ability to cope.

If you do tend to fall into the negative, pessimistic, half-empty side of the fence, you may find the following section of interest.

Reframing

We all have choices as to whether we see things in a positive, neutral or negative light. Even when a mistake is made, there is always the option of learning from it, in which case the mistake could be seen as a useful gift.

If you wish to change and re-frame your perceptions in order to view something in a different way, you would first need to catch yourself in the act.

All of us have thoughts that come automatically into our heads, just as we often have set ways of doing things (or not doing things) without noticing. Yet if we grab hold of these automatics we can challenge them and change them.

Can you name 6 things/thoughts that are automatic to you that would be useful to change or challenge?

My automatics	Change/Challenge
For example: I always think I'm going to say something silly when I speak in public.	I never say anything silly when I speak in public, so this makes no sense to me.
1	
2	
3	
4	
5	
6	

Reframing exercise

We invite you now to have a look at some examples of possible reframing and see if you can add some of your own ideas.

Negative stance	Positive or neutral reframe
She always shouts at me.	It is incorrect to say she "always" shouts at me. I like her energy.
I fear the worst.	Whatever will be will be.
I don't know how to do this.	I will find out how to do this.
There isn't enough time.	
I can't stand to be around him.	
I'm sure I'm doing this wrong.	
They never invite me out.	
I can't cope with this.	
They don't listen to me.	
I'll never be as good as them.	
I can't bear to watch her die.	

If there can be some kind of conclusion to draw from this section, it may be that:

The people with the greater range of coping strategies are more likely to be able to prevent the harmful effects of stressors than those who are reliant on a few.

The type of coping strategies you draw on in times of need will depend on what's available to you, but also on what type of person you are and what type of relationship you have with yourself.

If you like yourself and are nice to yourself you may find it easier coming up with useful and non-judgemental strategies. Whereas, if you are hard on yourself you may have the following types of automatic (and unhelpful) thoughts:

"I should be able to get this done without having to ask anyone for help."
"I must not get upset because it is a sign of weakness."
"I ought to ring my mum every day even when it is the last thing I want to do."

The more we understand about ourselves the better equipped we will be for life events that are distressing and stressful.

The oscillating self

The definition of oscillate is to swing back and forth, like a pendulum. As human beings – providing we don't restrict ourselves – we have the ability to oscillate from one state to another as a means of helping us to cope in different situations.

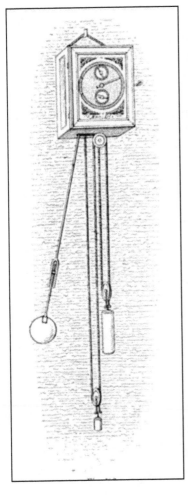

We are nice to our neighbour one minute and then horrible to the postman the next.

We weigh up arguments from different perspectives.

Sometimes we talk to ourselves, sometimes we do not

We can act so childishly, yet at other times be perfectly sensible.

We drink alcohol or take drugs, and another side of us comes out to play.

We sometimes save our tears for when we are alone and safe.

We find random opportunities to dump our frustrations on other people.

Maybe we are far more resourceful than we think we are.

PART 3.

Different types of coping strategies

Below is an incomplete A–Z list of strategies that have helped people (for better or worse) to cope with immediate, medium-term or long-term stresses and distresses.

a. Sleep

Getting good quality and regular sleep can be the difference between health and ill-health, coping and not-coping.

b. Breathing

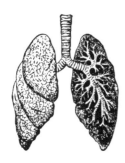

We often tense up in stressful situations, reducing the intake of air rather than the much more beneficial method of breathing deeply. Breathing can give us clarity, helping to relax us and release stuck emotions.

c. Laughter

What is it about the act of laughing that has the power to alter our mood and make our brains and body feel lighter?

15

d. Voice

Talking, singing, telling stories, screaming, wailing, yelping, howling and growling. Many people find using the full range of their voice both rewarding and liberating.

e. Touch

We all need physical contact. We can get this from being stroked or having a massage. We can also self-soothe through brushing our hair or applying facial cream. For relief and comfort, you can also tap different parts of your body such as the thymus gland in your neck.

f. Stimulants

Some people use drugs of this type in order to function, to be more alert, to enhance their mood and attain bursts of short-term pleasure.

g. Depressants

These reduce stimulation, calm us, slow down our heart rate and help us to relax and get us to sleep.

h. Music and sound

One of the most powerful ways in which we can alter or enhance our mood is through sounds – rhythms, beats, melodies, harmonies – that sympathetically match our own bodily vibrations.

i. Recovery bag items

These are things we carry around that we can use at any time to help us recover from stress. Items may include a phone, a book, a chocolate bar, water, etc.

j. Repetitive movements

There is scientific evidence that performing repetitive or rhythmic actions has the ability to lower blood pressure and tension in our muscles: whether it be knitting, sewing, rocking, running, colouring in, etc.

k. Self-harm/self-injury

While the words themselves may sound destructive, many people use methods such as cutting, ice cubes and elastic bands as a way of managing intense pain or of being able to re-connect with their world, when previously they have felt disconnected with themselves and their bodies.

l. Exercise

Sometimes a lack of physical action, of movement, of exerting energy, can have a negative impact on one's health. Exercise can give people a sense of health, purpose and achievement.

m. Sexual activity

Some people use sex as a coping strategy, by reaching an orgasm to help release pent-up frustrations and tensions and manage their emotions.

n. Dissociation

Some people survive trauma and abuse by separating or splitting from themselves, in order to avoid the horror of what is happening. This same action can also occur after the event(s), when a person feels they are being threatened in some way.

o. Avoidance

A simple way to cope is to avoid the problem: hide the bills and face the music later. Remain undecided so that you don't have to make the decision. Become anxious and fearful so you don't have to face the world. Become depressed so that you don't have to think or feel very much.

p. Work

Similar to (o), work can be a great way to avoid any other issues in your life – especially if you are in control of your work.

q. Isolation

Since most of the problems we face in life centre around relationships, hiding yourself away from them can alleviate that distress.

r. People

Being surrounded by people can be just the tonic you need. Being surrounded by supportive, non-judgemental, warm and loving people will be even better.

s. Animals and pets

Spending time with or forming relationships with animals and pets can be a safe and protective way of coping – as animals don't tend to give you a hard time!

t. Being in control

Some people get agitated when they are not in control. Some people who do not feel as though they have control over their life can use things such food and eating (or not eating) as a way of gaining control.

u. Aggression

For an immediate response to intense emotions and hostile environments, some people resort to aggressive behaviour. This can have the effect of transferring all of their frustrations onto other people, leaving themselves becalmed (until the consequences unfold).

v. Treats

Anything that is kind to yourself and can be considered a treat: such as soaking in a bath or walking in nature.

w. Escaping

Getting away from the epicentre of your distress can give you the time and space to think about what you might do next.

x. Shopping and spending money

Retail therapy is an immediate way of cheering yourself up.

y. Meditation, mantras, mindfulness, affirmations, silence and prayers

All of the above have the power to relax and to ground a person in the here and now. They can also provide comfort and strength and tap into resources of resilience.

z. Looking after someone else

Concentrating on the needs of other people can be a way of dealing with (or not dealing with) issues that are going on for you personally.

Different ways to de-stress

Below are some practical examples of ways in which we might de-stress, as chosen by the public at large. One thing you may notice about this list is that it doesn't acknowledge some of the less healthy ways in which we cope – those will come later!

99 healthy ways to de-stress

1. Meet a friend/friends
2. Paint, draw, write or create something
3. Find a hobby that occupies your mind, e.g. start collecting things
4. Swim or attend the gym
5. Read a book, a newspaper or a magazine
6. Listen to music/sounds
7. Create your own music/sounds
8. Watch a film or a TV programme
9. Listen to a radio programme/podcast/audiobook
10. Immerse yourself in nature
11. Take a walk
12. Find something pleasant to stroke – or be stroked
13. Soak in a bath
14. Meditate, pray, consciously relax or zone out, repeat a mantra, breathe, perform a yoga movement
15. Offload your frustrations on someone who can listen objectively
16. Watch animals
17. Walk a dog

18. Get more/less sleep
19. Plan, prepare and make a special meal
20. Do something that will make you feel good about yourself (maybe doing something for someone else, for your society or for humanity as a whole)
21. Write a letter to someone (or yourself) which you may or may not wish to send or keep
22. Write a list of things to do, then tick them off each time you get to achieve them
23. Start a diary
24. Share your thoughts and feelings
25. Switch off your phone and computer for a spell
26. Plan something you like/enjoy, either on your own or with friends/family
27. Plan a holiday or something in the future to look forward to
28. Dance or engage in movements around the room
29. Change the environment you are in
30. Go somewhere you have never been before
31. Explore your neighbourhood in more detail
32. Find ways to engage each of your senses
33. Go to a day/evening class
34. Learn something new
35. Find people who energise you or avoid people who sap your energy
36. Sit down
37. Stop doing what you are doing for a moment
38. Try to do nothing for a moment
39. Find wisdom in others, young and old alike
40. Experience different types of weather
41. Drink something that your body will savour
42. Eat something healthy or avoid something unhealthy
43. Do not do something you usually do and enjoy the moment of not doing it
44. Ask others what they do to de-stress
45. Do something you have never done before, be it something

small or large

46. Focus on finding ways to put a smile on your face, either by yourself or reaching out to other people
47. Organise an event
48. Do the thing you have avoided for a long time, to get it off your shoulders
49. Do something repetitive, like sewing, knitting or drumming
50. Immerse yourself in the colours that you like
52. Immerse yourself in the things that inspire you, such as art work, architecture, sculpture, etc.
53. Get some fresh air
54. Treat yourself to something, right now
55. Do something silly and childish
56. Do something that alters your appearance in some way
57. Have something to look forward to at the end of each day
58. Make up some characters to go into an ongoing story
59. Cuddle someone/something and be cuddled in return
60. Spend time with people who have a totally different take on life, such as children, young people, old people, spiritual/non-spiritual people
61. Break up your routine
62. Do something that takes you out of your comfort zone
63. Actively day-dream
64. Engage more in your dreams (i.e. by remembering them and writing them down)
65. Work out your family tree
66. Engage more in your imaginative side
67. Speak some words in a foreign language
68. Make up your own language
69. Sit in a café/park and watch the world go by
70. Tidy up a part of your home/life
71. Clean, slowly and deliberately
71. De-clutter your home one piece at a time
72. Alter the furniture in your house
73. Play a game, either by yourself or with others

74. Make a will
75. Hop on a bicycle
77. Go for a run
77. Set yourself a realistic challenge
78. Practice saying "no" or "yes" more often, if you are aware that you tilt one way more than the other
79. Rehearse in your mind any future situation that may make you anxious
80. Become part of a support group
81. Volunteer your time to a meaningful cause
82. Find affirmations that can work for you at any time of the day
83. Slow down/speed up
84. Experience what it is like to be bored – and what happens as a result of being bored
85. Engage more/less in your spiritual side
86. Work out what things you need to hand in order to de-stress when you are out and about
87. Keep objects of comfort close by
88. Learn a poem off by heart, so that you can recite it (in your head or aloud) at any moment in time
89. Visualise something calming, pleasant
90. Find somewhere that is quiet and peaceful to go to when you need to
91. Design a plan of action for when stress comes your way
92. Grow a plant/flower from seed
93. Have sex/make love
94. Massage yourself or receive a massage
95. Look at the changing sky at different times of the day
96. Wear something on your body to remind you to look after yourself (such as a badge or a brooch)
97. Find something that will take your breath away
98. Find a way to make another person smile
99. Find a rescue remedy that you can turn to in an emergency

Less healthy ways to de-stress

Some ways of coping/surviving can create their own set of problems. The list below is not designed to make you feel guilty or ashamed if you use any of them. It is more about keeping things real and having an open and honest dialogue with yourself about the nature of your coping strategies.

100. Drugs
101. Alcohol
102. Smoking
103. Gambling
104. Addictions/compulsions/obsessions/impulsive behaviour
105. Over-eating/under-eating/eating disorders
106. Self-harm
107. Over-use of computer/internet
108. Risky sex/pornography
109. Power and control over others
110. Anger/aggression/road rage/violence
111. Attempting suicide

Coping diversions

Can you name some of the coping strategies you use that stop you moving forward in your life? It could be that they take you on a detour, or that they lead you astray, or round and round or, worse, that they bring you to a dead-end.

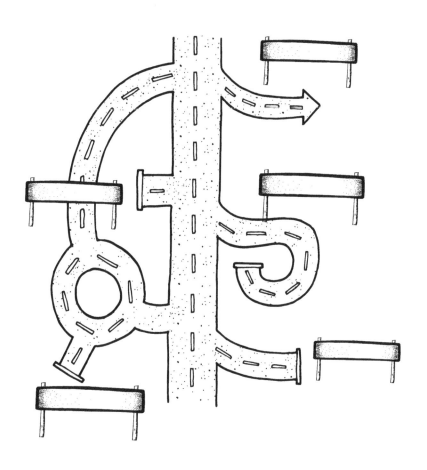

Matching coping strategies to issues

It's all very well looking at coping strategies on their own, but it might be more useful to find out exactly what we are trying to cope with…

Do any of these issues apply to you?

Alienation	Lack of resilience	Overwhelmed
Estrangement	Unresolved childhood issues	Depression
Stress	Work	Anxiety
Domestic abuse	Health	Isolation
Disempowerment	Toxic relationships	Loss
Identity	Lack of self-worth	Trauma
Abuse	Shame	Addictions
Grief	Family breakdown	Guilt

What coping strategy might you be using to deal with your present issues? Could there be an alternative way of coping?

Issue	Current coping	Alternative coping

Warning signs and triggers

What are the signs that you aren't coping very well?
What is likely to trigger you having a dip in your wellness?

Below are some suggestions, followed by an opportunity for you to write down your own answers.

Possible warning signs

- A change in behaviour, routine or habits.
- A loss of humour, energy, enjoyment, motivation.
- Increased heart rate. Restlessness. Unease. Tension. Sweating. Nervousness. Disorientation. Avoidance. Distraction. Irritability. Defensiveness. Anger and aggression.
- A sense of dread, fear, worry.
- A change in eating/sleeping pattern, hygiene.
- Criticism of self – and others.

My warning signs	What strategy can I use?

Possible triggers

- Financial worries
- Bumping into an ex-partner
- Drugs/alcohol
- Grief/anniversary of a loss/death
- Physical illness
- Harassment/bullying/victimisation
- Disempowerment/alienation/oppression
- Being judged/criticized
- Family breakdown/arguments
- Overwhelmed by work/exams

My triggers	What strategy can I use?

Too late

If you are overwhelmed by stress, if you are under tremendous amounts of pressure, or if you have become a crazy mule, then it's likely to be too late to make any rational, sensible and meaningful decision(s). So how about you don't even try? Instead, how about you:

- Wait for a moment of calm and clarity
- Wait until you are out of the hostile environment
- Plan and prepare for the next wave of stress in advance of it happening again

Planning, preparation and pro-activity

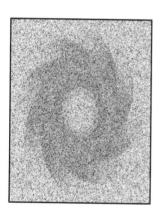

If you know you're entering into a vortex of stress/distress and you have some time on your side, how about you take steps to plan and prepare for the onset, before you lose the ability to think clearly? Instead of leaving things to chance, or hoping other people will take responsibility for your well-being, perhaps you can take a pen and paper and execute your own plan of action.

A plan of action could be a moment-by-moment approach, or it could be day by day. It could involve finding out who will be around to help you and what times they can commit to, or it could be working out what things you need and when you need them. It may also include finding out if there are any pockets of down-time, or treats, available to you. [See Part 9 for more details].

Questions about coping

Q: How would you describe your general state of mind at present?

A:

Q: Over the past three months, how stressed have you been compared to the previous three months?

A:

Q: How important is it for you to be in control of things?

A:

Q: How important to your well-being is having a relatively tidy environment?

A:

Q: On a continuum between being tidy and being cluttered, where would you put yourself?

Tidy   Cluttered

←——————————————————————————————→

Q: On a continuum between being organised and disorganised where would you put yourself?

Organised   Disorganised

←——————————————————————————————→

Q: If one of your places of being (e.g. home/office/college) starts to become a hostile environment, do you have another place to go to de-stress?
A:

Q: How good are you at switching off?
A:

Q: Do holidays relax you or make you tense?
A:

What questions would be important to ask yourself at this moment in time? Do you have the beginnings of an answer?

Q:
A:

Q:
A:

Q:
A:

Q:
A:

Coping strategy compass #1

You are now invited to plot your own coping strategies into the four quadrants of the compass. Once you have done this, have a look to see if your methods of coping are evenly spread out or whether you would benefit from targeting a certain quadrant with more strategies.

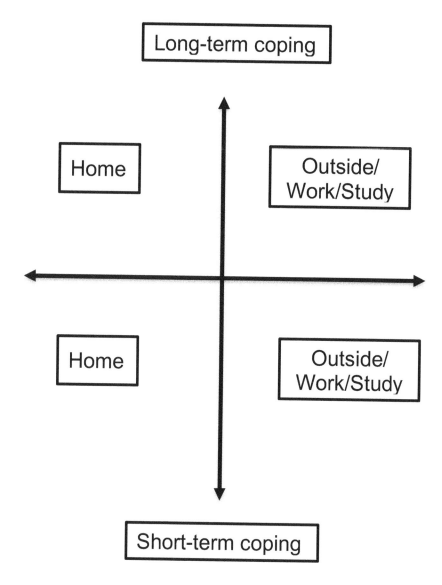

Coping strategy compass #2

Try to be as honest with yourself as you can when plotting this compass. Once you have done the exercise, have a look to see if you're okay with how it looks or whether you would like to change it in some way.

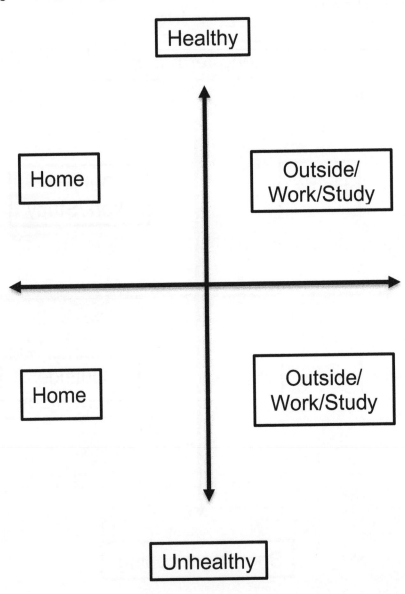

PART 4.

The recovery bag

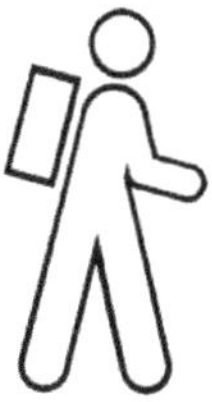

When you leave your home and go out into the world, do you take a bag with you? If you do, what do you put in this bag? Does your bag contain any items that might come to your aid – if and when you need them?

The notion of carrying a "recovery bag" around with you is to help keep you safe and to help you de-stress when a situation arises, with or without warning.

We are now going to hand you over to Karen, who is going to unpack the items in her bag for you and give a rationale for carrying each of them.

Coping strategy case study: the worrier's recovery bag

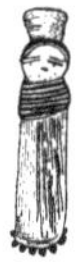

"Hi, my name is Karen. I am 45 years old and I have been consciously carrying things in my recovery bag for around 10 years now.

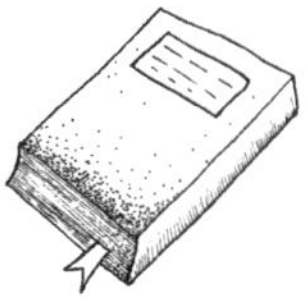

"I get bored very easily – like really, really bored – so now I always take a book with me when I go out, along with a couple of pages of puzzles, a pen and a small note pad, in case I have an idea that I will forget if I don't write it down at once, or in case I want to doodle or draw something.

"A bottle of water is a must for me, as is a snack bar for some energy and an emergency chocolate, in case I'm ever feeling low and need a bit of comfort. Sometimes, instead of chocolate, I will pack a hand cream that I can use to soothe myself if I need a bit of TLC.

"I also carry a phone and a charger with me at all times, a small amount of loose change, my keys, an asthma inhaler, a photo of my daughters, a small make-up bag, a packet of tissues; and a stress ball.

"As I'm a big worrier, I like to have access to music, 24/7. As long as there is music, there is always a chance I can get myself to calm down.

"You may think that all of this weighs a ton, but it is surprisingly compact and light – or maybe I'm just used to it now. My final item is my worry doll. It is hand-made, from Guatemala. It stays with me at all times (I have 10 of them, just in case I lose one). At night, I put her under my pillow and she takes my worries away. During the day, I pick her up from time to time and hold her in my hand and silently tell her my anxieties. She's great."

My recovery bag

If you were to design your own recovery bag, what would you put in it?

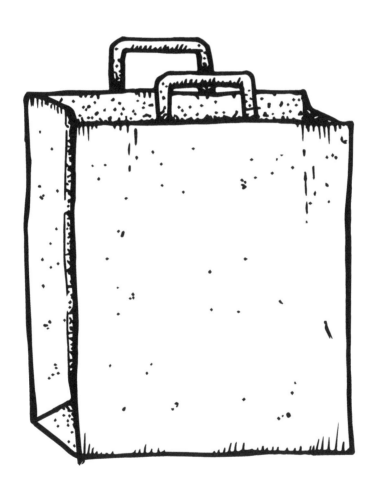

Letting go

[Based on a short story by Susan Clegg]

Margaret always carried a bag around with her. The bag was very important because it had been handed down to her by her mother, who in turn had been bought the bag by her own mother. The contents of the bag were also very important to Margaret. She had some very special mementos of her life in this bag.

One day as Margaret was walking along a street she heard a noise right behind her, and as she turned around with a start, her bag was expertly snatched from her by a woman – who was running down the street with the bag under her arm.

"No!" Margaret shouts. "You can't take that! That is my bag!"

Margaret gave chase. She ran and ran after her bag as though her life depended on it. As she ran she gained more and more speed. As she ran she shouted louder and louder, "Give me back my bag! It's a very important bag!"

The thief, whose name was Jemma, looked behind her and saw the determination on Margaret's face. Jemma was struck at that moment by how ugly and twisted Margaret's face was. She was thinking it was a horrible face for anyone to have to make. She pitied Margaret, and even though she could've easily out-run Margaret, she decided she didn't want the bag anymore – and she certainly didn't want anything more to do with Margaret. So Jemma threw the bag high into the air and crossed to the other side of the road and around the corner.

Margaret watched as the bag sailed up in the air. Margaret was so close she could have easily caught it, but she didn't. Instead, she let the bag crash-land on the floor. She then jumped over the bag, crossed the road and turned the corner.

Jemma, who was now strolling away from the scene of her crime, was in disbelief when she saw Margaret come racing up behind her, without her precious bag. Margaret's face now looked completely different. Tears were streaming down her face and she was laughing at the same time. It was like a huge weight had been lifted from her shoulders. "Thank you," Margaret said as she ran past Jemma. "Thank you so much."

| Q: What is your immediate reaction to this story? |
| A: |

| Q: What do you think has happened to Margaret during the course of this episode? |
| A: |

| Q: Do you identify with any elements of this story? |
| A: |

| Q: What would you like to let go of? |
| A: |

PART 5.

Close-up on 7 ways of coping

In this section, we will be looking at the art of breathing, sleeping, music, ways to switch off the brain, and the art of decluttering as well as laughter and stomach bacteria!

(i). Breathing

When we need to breathe the most, like when we are stressed, or stuck in a rut, or up a height, we tend to do the opposite. We hold our breath, clench our hands, tense our bodies. Yet if we did remember to breathe during these moments, we would find that there are lot more possibilities open to us, as well as greater clarity of thought, which can help us to de-stress or de-escalate a situation.

Conversely, taking more breaths than you usually would (otherwise known as shallow breathing or hyperventilating) is often developed during an anxiety attack, which only serves to heighten the intensity of the anxiety and perpetuate the fear that you are out of control. Yet if there was a way of taking control of our breathing, then perhaps we could help to settle ourselves in times of difficulty.

Breathing through the nose

Unless there is a good reason not to do so, the general wisdom it that it is healthier to breathe through your nostrils than it is to breathe through your mouth (with the exception of when you are undertaking vigorous physical exercise). For one, nasal breathing allows the lungs to absorb greater amounts of oxygen. It also warms up the air to body temperature and filters out unwanted particles.

If you mouth-breathe through force of habit alone, perhaps you may wish to invest time in swapping over to the nose.

Conscious breathing

The act of conscious breathing is simply about bringing the (normally) automatic function of breathing into your awareness, so that you can alter the flow and the rate of air going back and forth into our lungs.

The benefits of deeper conscious breathing into the lungs, for certain periods of time, are many. Here are some examples:
- Increased energy levels
- Released muscle tension and stress
- Relaxed nervous system
- Oxygenated organs

The benefits of slower conscious breathing include:
- Reduced anxiety and arousal
- Improved sleep

- Reduced heart rate
- Lower levels of adrenalin(e)

Collectively conscious breathing can help:
- Release suppressed emotions
- Manage pain
- Manage intense emotions, such as anger and guilt
- Recover from a trauma
- Prevent illness
- Increase self-control and resilience

Below are some exercises to get you actively engaged in your breathing. If you research more into this subject you will also see the connection breathing has with other disciplines, such as yoga, meditation and mindfulness.

Breathing exercise #1

1. Inhale through your nose and down into your belly for 3 beats.
2. Hold your breath for 3 beats.
3. Release your breath for 3 beats.

Repeat steps for up to five minutes.
Increase the beats to 4 and then 5 if you can.
Change the stages if you wish, so that you start with 1, move to 3 then 2 then back to 1 again.

Breathing exercise #2

1. Lie down in a comfortable position
2. Rest your hand just below your rib cage.
3. Inhale and exhale (x10) so that your hands experience the rise and fall of your belly.
4. Rest your hands on the sides of your rib cage.
5. Inhale and exhale (x10) so that your hands experience the rise and fall of your rib cage.
6. Rest your hands above your rib cage, just below your shoulder blades.

7. Inhale and exhale (x10) while focusing on the areas where your hands are resting. (You may or may not experience a gentle movement in this area.)

Breathing exercise #3

1. Take it in turn to press a finger down on each side of your nostril so that your breath is being channelled up and down one side of your nose at a time. Focus your awareness on the inhalation and exhalation through each nostril.
2. See if you can do the above exercise (1.) by concentrating on each nostril in turn without the use of a finger.

Breathing exercise #4

1. Place your hands on your belly. Inhale through the nose slowly until the belly expands like a balloon.
2. Release the air through the mouth in one go.

Breathing exercise #5

1. Lie down with your hands by your side and close your eyes.
2. Bring your awareness to your feet.
3. Breathe in slowly.
4. As you release the breath, imagine, sense or visualise the air brushing past your feet before leaving your body.
5. Pick another part of the body to focus on and repeat steps 3 and 4. Do this for as many parts of your body as you wish.
6. End the exercise by slowly opening your eyes and bringing your awareness back into the room.

(ii). Sleep

Sleep is one of the most important things our bodies need in order to stay healthy. A good night's sleep can also help us to cope with so many things that life throws at us. So, please, please, please, do make it your number-one priority to maintain or improve your sleep in whichever ways you can.

You may suffer from poor sleep, either through lack of self-care or the environment you are in, or you may have lost the ability to switch off due to all sorts of circumstances.

Pain, ruminations, work, addictions, worries, lack of structure and routine, life changes, sound, light, hormonal changes, grief, depression and nightmares are just some of the ways in which we can be thrown out of kilter. This may have gone on for weeks or months or years. No matter how difficult you think it may be, we would still recommend that you explore sleep afresh, from a Self Detective perspective.

Exploratory sleep questions

What does the word *sleep* mean to you? Do you enjoy it? Fear it? Would it help you to embrace the world of sleep and all that it gives to you: e.g. a chance for the body to repair itself and a chance for the brain to process information from the day? Would it help you to understand the mechanics of sleep?

When is your sleep at its poorest? What features and conditions can provide you with a higher quality of sleep?
Do you avoid having to deal with sleep and then just tolerate sleeplessness when it arrives?

What if sleep was the most important function of your day? What steps might you take in the run-up to sleep in order to get the most out of it? What if you planned for your sleep in the full knowledge of what has worked best for you in the past and what hasn't worked and what you might be able to change and what, realistically, you cannot? What if you gave yourself permission to explore the whole length and breadth of your sleep, ruling nothing in and nothing out? Are you willing to try new approaches to sleep?

Some people

Some people feel the need to be in control at all times and do not like the transitional moment between wakefulness and sleep. They fight it and fight it until they can no longer remain awake. Yet what would it be like not to fight it? To accept the paradox that being too much in control can make you out of control? Can the transition be made easier to deal with by letting go of your wakefulness on your own terms and in your own way?

Some people try too hard. Yet you don't get to sleep by forcing yourself to sleep. You get to sleep by acknowledging how tired you are.

Some people are unable to get to sleep because they are not in the present moment. They are either thinking about what has happened in the past or they are thinking about what may happen in the future. If this is the case, then some breathing exercises may help them back into the here and now.

Some people curse themselves with a negative narrative: "I have trouble getting to sleep" or "I am a poor sleeper" (as though this defines you as a person). How about a different approach instead, something along the lines of "I am open to ways to improve my sleep"?

Some people dislike change.
How much are you prepared to change?

Sometimes there is a clear-cut solution to the problem of sleep, yet we don't act on it because we worry about the consequences. For example, if we sleep with another person and they keep us awake by their snoring or their movements in the night, a solution would be to sleep apart or use ear plugs.

Good sleep practice

1. Create the best and most conducive sleep environment you possibly can. With every possible detail considered, down to the amount of light you have, the colour of the walls and the colour of the lights, the bedding not too hot, not too cold, the lack of creases on your sheets, smells or no smells, noise or no noise, temperature, objects you may or may not need at hand (Music. Radio. Scent. Eye mask. Book. Notepad and pen. Ear plugs.) In essence, you are decluttering your room and turning it into a sacred space, geared up as much as it can to providing you with what you might need.

2. Set up a pre-sleep routine. This may involve, for example:

(i) Not eating or taking stimulants or stimulating yourself after a certain time in the evening.
(ii) Having a regular sleep-inducing night-time drink.
(iii) Giving yourself a period of time to decant your thoughts and put them to one side (ideally by writing them down or sharing them with another person).
(iv) Establishing a slow and deliberate bathroom routine.
(v) Winding down at the same time every night.
(vi) Place a worry doll under your pillow.

3. Undertake a breathing exercise sitting on the bed or lying on top of the bed or while lying inside the bed.

4. Have a mantra to repeat to help you shift away from your brain noise.

5. Use breathing exercises to help to ground yourself in the here and now moment.

My own pre-sleep routine

What might your own ideal approach to sleep look like?

Time/duration	Pre-sleep activity

My sleep log

Would it be useful to keep a log of all the interventions you use to help with your sleep so far?

Action	Did it work? (Y/N)	Notes

(iii). Music and sound

The definition of **resonance** is when the vibrations of one external force cause another to move in a rhythmic way. This is more likely to happen if the two forces share a similar, natural frequency.

Finding types of music and sound that match our own vibrations – that can resonate with us at an atomic level – is of real importance to our well-being. Similarly, cutting out music and sounds that are unpleasant, upsetting, clashing and disharmonious (otherwise known as **dissonance**) can also be of great benefit to us.

Listening to music has all sorts of therapeutic benefits. It reduces stress and anxiety levels. It can improve your mood, your heart rate and your blood pressure. Music helps to develop cognitive skills such as attention and memory. It can also give you a sense of control, by providing you with a sense of the familiar and a grounding in reality when you feel disconnected. It also influences your metabolism, sleep, respiration and helps reduces fatigue.

Q: How do we know which sounds make us well and which make us ill?
A: We find out. We go on a journey of discovery. We look for clues. We start with what we already know.

Different types of music

It may be worth splitting music into sub-sections.

If we are interested in being able to study and concentrate or to use music to help us sleep, **monophonic** music works wonders. Monophonic music contains one melodic line without the harmony, for example Gregorian chanting. This type of music helps to preoccupy our subconscious mind, so that we can focus our attention elsewhere.

Polyphonic music contains multiple instruments, or voices and harmonies, that are played at the same time, such as Johann Pachelbel's *Canon*. Polyphonic music is complex and demands concentration; it can completely absorb us, challenge us, and plant all sorts of imagery into our subconscious that in turn can stimulate creativity.

Homophonic is where vocals and instruments complement a dominant rhythm or repetitive beat, and which constitutes most pop music. For many Western people this music is very straightforward and easy to grasp as it played everywhere. It is the music that is most likely to make you dance.

Heterophonies can be heard in bluegrass and Cajun and in many non-Western types of music. Here there is one melody played out by two instruments (say fiddle and banjo) at the same time, without necessarily being perfectly synchronised, which creates a natural texture to the sound.

Polyrhythms. This is where two or more separate rhythms combine and conflict with one another. The origins of this music are African. If played over a long period of time, the effects of this music can be hypnotic and transcendental.

Would it be useful to you to listen to music that you have never heard before, to find out if it has an impact on your well-being?

Music and sound questions

Q: What types of music do you enjoy?
A:
Q: What sounds do you enjoy?
A:
Q: Is there a common theme to your choice of music and sound? E.g. the pitch, the frequency, the rhythm?
A:
Q; Is there a musical instrument that you particularly like?
A:
Q: What type of voices/singers do you like?
A:
Q: What music do you not enjoy?
A:
Q: What sounds do you not enjoy?
A:
Q: Is there a common theme to your dislike of the music and sounds? E.g. the pitch, the frequency, the rhythm?
A:
Q: Is there a musical instrument that you dislike the sound of?
A:
Q: What type of voices/singers do you most dislike?
A:
Q: Do you reach for music when you are upset?
A:

Q: In relation to sound, what environment do you work best in?
A:
Q: What songs make you want to dance?
A:
Q: What songs would you chose for your own funeral?
A:
Q: Do songs need to have a meaning for you before you can engage with them?
A:
Q: How aware are you of everyday sounds in general?
A:
Q: Which sounds are you more aware of than others?
A:
Q: Are you more likely to notice pleasant sounds or irritating sounds?
A:

Resonance exercises

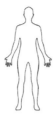

1. Using only yourself and your own body, find ways of making sounds that resonate with you.

2. Using items from your own home, find ways of making sounds that you like.

3. Take a walk in your neighbourhood, listen out for sounds that resonate with you.

4. When you are away from your natural habitat, listen out for new sounds that you may like.

5. If you do find sounds that you like, make a note of them (or record them) so that you can produce or hear the sound whenever you need to.

My resonance discovery notes:

Iso-moodic principle

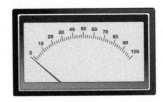

According to the principles of music therapy you can change your mood, as well as calm your body, by listening to a certain number of songs in a certain order or sequence, so as to transport you, step by step, into whichever mood you want to go to.

> Iso-moodic principle is "a technique by which music is matched with the mood, then gradually altered to affect the desired mood state. This technique can also be used to affect physiological responses such as heart rate and blood pressure."
>
> William B. Davis, Kate E. Gfeller, Michael Thaut, authors of *An Introduction to Music Therapy*.

To some people this idea may seem somewhat counter-intuitive. They may ask, "If I'm in a bad mood and I want cheering up, why would I want to play a song that is miserable? Why not play something that is happy?" To which the answer would be: playing a happy song when you are miserable will not have any meaningful effect. Only by matching music to your mood do you then get to alter it, step by step.

So, for example, if you wanted to move from angry to happy, you may need to find music (or sounds) that takes you along the following pathway:

Angry -- Serious -- Majestic -- Passionate -- Happy
or
Angry -- Sentimental -- Serene -- Playful -- Happy

In order to use this concept as a coping strategy, you will need to set up a whole host of playlists or categories that are unique to you and your moods. This may require a fair amount of trial and error. You can either start the matching process (i) by finding out which music/sounds resonate with your current mood at any given time or (ii) by playing lots of different types of music/sounds and finding out what mood they put you in.

The chart below is incomplete. You may wish to add your own mood words at the bottom, along with the matching sound/music. Put down as many tunes or noises as you want.

My mood	My matching music/sounds playlist
Happy	
Playful	
Serene	
Dreamy	
Gloomy	
Serious	
Majestic	
Passionate	

My mood	My matching music/sounds playlist

The mood wheel

As a music psychologist, Kate Hevner devoted much of her professional career to exploring the therapeutic benefits of music. She created the mood wheel as an extension to the iso-moodic principle.

The mood wheel provides the user with 8 clusters of words/adjectives that are closely related to one another. Each of these clusters has two neighbouring groups of words, which have connections to each other. As a whole, these collections form a circle or a cycle, from 1 to 8. Each cluster will have a range of moods that are diagonally opposite and different from each other.

How to use the mood wheel (see the diagrams overleaf)

a. Using the descriptive words in each cluster, amass a number of songs and/or sounds that fits into each of your mood wheel's 8 segments. (These songs/playlists/soundtracks will ideally be available to you in your home as well as when you are out and about).
b. Whenever you want to change your mood, you will need to know which number you are currently in and which number you want to get to. For example, 2 to 7 or 3 to 4 or 5 to 1. You will also have the choice of going around the mood wheel clockwise or anti-clockwise.
c. Play a song (or multiple songs) from the mood cluster you are in. Then, play a song or songs from the neighbouring cluster and so on until you get to the music that matches the mood you want.
d. You have now (hopefully) arrived at your chosen mood!

So, for example, I am currently in a playful mood, which puts me into cluster 5, yet I want to be serious (1). I am going to play songs in an anti-clockwise fashion from (5) (6) (7) (8) before arriving at (1).

Mood wheel illustration

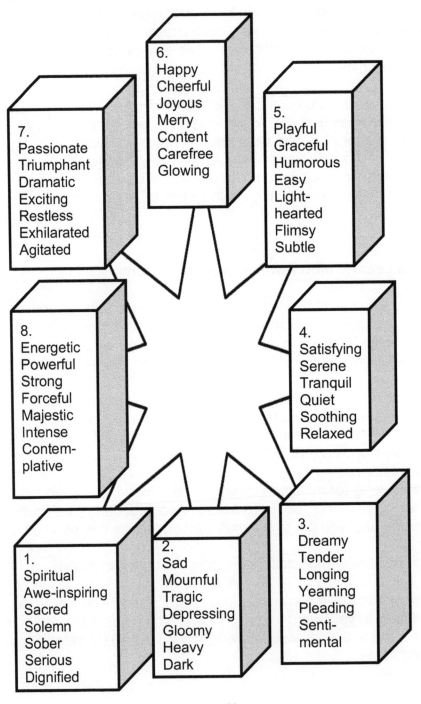

My mood wheel
Using the adjectives from the mood wheel illustration, match
your own songs and sounds to each of your 8 mood clusters.

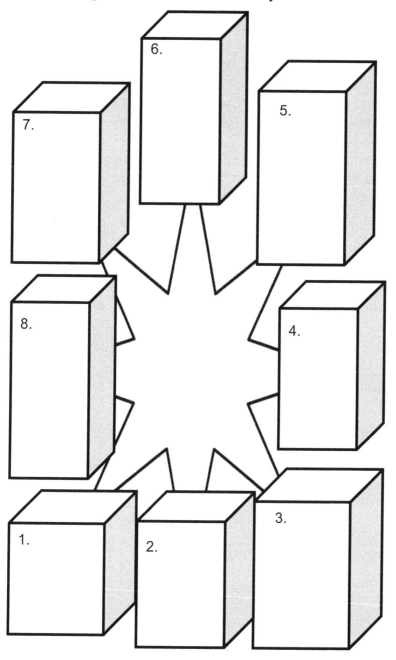

(iv). Switching off the brain (and focusing elsewhere)

Bodywork

It's all very well focusing on our thoughts, feelings and actions for certain aspects of our lives, but if we have some form of trauma or emotional blockage or a general ailment within our physical body, we would likely need a new approach. This is where bodywork comes in. Not only can it help to release stresses and distresses, it can also improve posture and energy levels as well as bringing the mind and the body closer together.

Below is an incomplete list of bodywork practices for you to investigate further if you so wish. Some of these interventions involve touch, while others do not.

Alexander technique	Visceral manipulation	Feldenkrais method	Hydro-therapy
Ortho-Bionomy	Polarity therapy	Deep tissue massage	Pranic healing
Craniosacral therapy	Bowen therapy	Rosen method	Aston-Patterning
Breema	Biofeedback	Trager work	Gua sha
One Light Healing Touch	Neuro-muscular re-programming	Connective tissue massage	Flotation re-patterning
Lymphatic massage	Marma therapy	Myofascial release	Jin Shin Jyutsu
Qigong	Lomi work	Rolfing	Reiki
Reflexology	Amanae	Watsu	Hellerwork
Breath perception	Trigger Point therapy	Soft tissue release	Swedish massage
Bioenergy	Aromatherapy	Hypno-therapy	Iridology
Thai massage	Acupressure	Hot stone massage	Oncology massage

Mantra

If you wish to take a break from the endless thought-traffic generated by a noisy brain, having your own mantra may be a useful tool for you.

A mantra, for SD purposes, is a nonsensical word or series of words that form a phrase that can either be spoken aloud or inside the head, over and over again, in order to bring about peace and tranquillity.

A suggestion to begin with is to practise this for 5 minutes in the morning and 5 minutes at night, as well as to use it on an as-and-when basis.

If you are stuck for a mantra, you would be welcome to pick one of these (providing the words/phrases don't have any meaning for you that will distract you in any way):

Chu Ku Ley Mar   Jem Nay Seer Fah
Sumja Bey Um   Lum Suu Kin Boo
Pel Naa Seylah   Sil Hah Joa Vey
Bu Ray Zim Tah   Chay Woo Baydah

Otherwise, you could always ask someone to come up with a mantra for you, or you could create your own one. Alternatively, you could look into the mantras from yoga, Hinduism, Sikhism and Buddhism, starting with the sacred sound of *Om*.

Affirmations

An affirmation is a word, phrase or quote that, if remembered, can be brought into focus at any moment in time to help you come through a difficult situation or to give you a boost of self-belief. There is also a notion that if you say an affirmation for long enough, you will be able to assimilate its meaning into your own being.

For an affirmation to work it needs to be meaningful to the person saying it. For example:

"I will not give up, as I haven't tried all the options yet."

This affirmation could be effective if you would benefit from a good dose of conviction in order to keep on keeping on. However, if your hopelessness is stronger than your hope, the affirmation is likely to be counter-productive.

The following affirmations are matched to a theme. If you like any of them, take them and repeat them over and over until they are well and truly inside your head. If you can make up your own affirmations, all the better.

Self-determination
"I always do the best for myself, no matter what."

When you are lacking motivation for the day ahead
"I will walk into the day and I will find something worthwhile within it."

When you are fearful of what might happen
"I trust myself and my abilities."

Facing a problem
"I can get through this. This is not the end of the world."

Difficulty sleeping
"I give myself permission to end my thoughts for the day and seek peace in sleep."

When you are angry
"I take full responsibility for myself and my actions."

When your self-esteem has been knocked by someone else
"I believe in myself. I know how amazing I am."

When you are sad and alone
"I know this is a temporary state. I know there are people out there who care for me."

My own affirmations

Theme:
"

Theme:
"

Theme:
"

Self detective tactile boxes

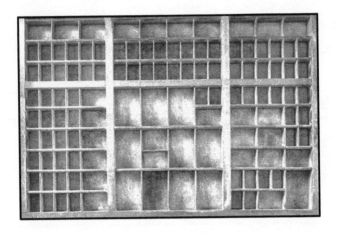

Instructions:

1. Find a box or storage container and divide it into many different sub-sections. If you can find an old printer's wooden box, so much the better.
2. Fill the box with all sorts of textures such as:

Sandpaper	Leaves	Plastic	Wood	Sponge
Wire	Nuts/bolts	Rubber	Leather	Clay
Plasticine	Rock	Wool	Sand	Metal

3. Touch each object in turn and see if a certain type of tactile stimulation matches your mood, or brings you comfort, or helps to ground you in some way.
4. Use the tactile box as and when you feel the need.
5. If you recognise which types of textures/materials/ fabrics best match your needs, you could start to carry them around with you.

Silence: inactivity, disengagement and quietness

Our senses are being constantly bombarded with information. What would it be like to be silent for a moment, without any purposeful activity going on inside your brain, without any need or urge to engage in the outside world? To some people this may sound quite boring or depressing, while to others it may be a lifeline out of the stresses and strains of being constantly on the go.

Often people who have mastered the art of slowing down and becoming still for periods of time find they are less tired, more alert and generally feel more energetic. Others, who practise the art of silence, either alone or as a group, for longer periods of time, experience a whole raft of 'happenings' inside themselves, such as a release of tension and an outpouring of emotion.

Some people, however, fall at the first hurdle of silence. They *try* to find silence or they *try* and block out the noise. Or they *try* to get from A to B in one fell swoop, rather than have the experience of the journey. They fail because their mind is all-seeing and all-knowing when it comes to its own affairs. It resists the silence by filling the void with any old junk. That is when the people give up and say, "No, this is not for me."

Other people, though, who have more perseverance and no expectations, who don't force themselves to stop thinking, who are up for the journey and are happy to commit themselves to a certain amount of time each day in the pursuit of quietness, are more likely to be rewarded with the calmness and tranquillity that they seek.

If you are serious about silence, could you answer the following questions?

Q: Realistically, if I wanted to make a go of this, would I?
Q: Realistically, could I do this on my own or would I need to book a course or a retreat with other people?
Q: If I am to do this on my own, when in the day could I do it, where would I do it and for how long?
Q: Would a meditational app be of use to me?

Being in the present moment

There is only one moment, and that is right here, right now.

If you are dwelling on things from the past or endlessly fretting on what may happen in the future, it is little wonder that you are stressed. So surely any means of getting you to have more and more moments where you are rooted to the here and now can only be a good thing?

The perceived wisdom of how to achieve this state of being is to be **slow**, **aware**, **deliberate** and **purposeful** in whatever kind of action you may wish to do.

Type "mindfulness" or "mindfulness exercises" into a search engine and you will get a million and one suggestions as to how to achieve this aim. So maybe all you need to do to help yourself on your way is to work out what actions you would like to be mindful of, and then seek them out online. The exercise could involve eating or drinking, it could be around your breathing or your skin or your body as a whole. It could be connected to driving or cycling or walking or swimming. It could involve looking, listening, touching, tasting, smelling. It could pretty much be about anything and everything. The question is: where would you like to start?

Body tapping

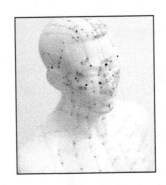

According to Chinese traditional medicine, meridian points on our body are channels of energy that can sometimes get blocked or shut down in times of upheaval and disturbance within the body and mind. However, when these points are stimulated, the flow of energy can be repaired. In Western medicine, this is likely to be referred to as the nervous system.

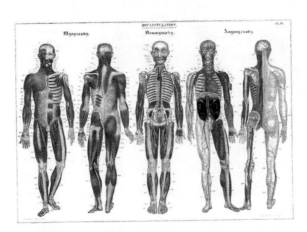

Emotional Freedom Technique (alongside Meridian Tapping Techniques), otherwise known as 'tapping', encourages us to use our own hands and fingers to apply small amount of pressure on certain meridian points in order to significantly reduce the effects of, among other things, cortisol. Cortisol is the stress hormone that can flood our body when the part of the brain called the amygdala perceives there to be a threat.

Below are three illustrations of where the meridian points are, followed by an exercise to get you started.

Meridian points

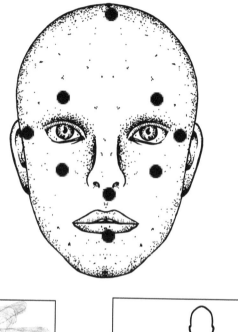

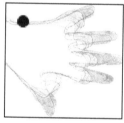 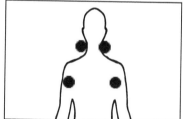

- Top of head
- Eyebrows
- Side of eyes
- Underneath the eyes
- Under the nose
- Chin
- Collarbone
- Underneath the arms
- Outer edge of the palm (opposite the thumb)

Tapping exercise #1

1. Focus your mind on a problem or issue that you have (whether it be physical, emotional or cognitive).
2. Give this matter a score out of ten, where 10 is highly intense and distressing and where 0 is of low intensity and of no concern.
3. Using two or three fingers, tap on each of the meridian points for around 5 seconds at a time.
4. Return to the problem or issue you identified.
5. Give this matter a score out of 10.

If the intensity has decreased, then perhaps tapping can become a regular feature for you. If the intensity has not decreased yet you feel better for having undertaken the exercise, then again you may wish to continue doing so.

NB. There are plenty of tutorials, exercises and information about tapping online.

(v). De-cluttering

If your home is overrun because more things are coming in than are going out, you may benefit from making a pledge to yourself to readjust the balance and focus some of your energy on removing items either to the bin or to be recycled. Hopefully such an act will provide you with the following benefits:

- More structure
- More control
- More space to breathe
- Less chaos
- Less stress
- A sense of achievement

De-cluttering contract to myself

I will remove ….. items a day/week/month for the next …… week/month/year starting on …… and ending on ………

Signed………………….
Date………
Witnessed by …………………….
Date……...

(vi). Laughter

If the act of laughing is good for you – and a lot of people seem to think it is – could you make a conscious effort to do it more often? Could you actively find things that are humorous or find ways in which your body is in a pleasurable state of fits and convulsions?

This could involve setting time aside to see a funny film, or to watch a comedian, or listen to comedy on the radio. If you were more serious about laughter, it could be something that you perform as a matter of routine, either on your own or in a group of people.

One thing that may stop us from letting go of ourselves and giving in to laughter is being self-conscious or feeling silly or stupid for doing so. Nonetheless, if we don't give it a try, how will we ever know the benefits of what we are doing?

Possible ways to laugh

All of these suggestions can be undertaken either on your own, with someone else or as part of a wider group. (The advantage of laughing with other people is the contagious aspect of laughter.) These can be done singularly or combined; standing or seated; with or without a mirror. All of these possibilities require a willingness to want to laugh for the good of your health. If you are resistant or just not in the mood, then perhaps it is better not to do it at that moment in time. By all means fake-laugh if it helps you get to the real stuff. Once you are up and running, find ways to stoke up, prolong and enhance the quality of the laughter.

- Pull a variety of absurd facial expressions
- Contort your face with your hands
- Form noises in your mouth and throat that are not usually part of your range
- Form and repeat words that amuse you
- Judder your shoulders
- Rub your tummy up and down
- Puff out your cheeks, blow a raspberry
- Mimic the mechanics of your usual laughter
- Mimic the laughter of an archetypal insane or evil person
- Snigger, gurgle, guffaw
- Make up nonsense words
- Find ways to gently poke fun at yourself
- Exaggerate ridiculous movements or dance routines
- Find ways to clown around
- Pretend to be someone else
- Pretend to be an animal or an alien or an object
- Imagine someone has let off a canister of laughing gas
- Sit on a whoopee cushion

(vii). Healthy bacteria

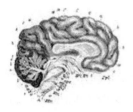

Our stomach is sometimes referred to as our second brain, due to the fact that as well as receiving messages, it also sends messages to the brain.

Inside our gut we have millions of neurons that communicate with billions of bacteria. How healthy the bacteria inside our tummy are goes some way to determining what type of signals our neurons send to the brain.

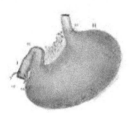

Bad bacteria from too much junk and processed food can create a toxic environment that can affect our mood, with higher levels of stress, depression and anxiety. Conversely good bacteria can help to reduce these things.

Below are some possible ways to improve the health and diversity of our stomach microbes:

- Fibrous food
- 'Live' yoghurt
- Plant-based food
- Fermented food
- A varied diet
- Probiotics (e.g. lactobacillus or bifidobacterium)

You are what you eat

PART 6.

The direction of wellness

Here are two very blunt questions for you to consider if you have ever been hurt, harmed or wronged.

Q: Can striving for **justice** (such as revenge, retribution, punishment, payback, retaliation) bring you **wellness**, or are they two different beasts altogether?

Similarly, if you have become a victim of someone or something...

Q: Can being in the state of **victimhood** give you **wellness**, or not?

The reason we ask these questions is that at Self Detective our only concern is your well-being and the well-being of others. If seeking justice or being in a passive victim-mode doesn't help your well-being or gets in the way of your wellness, then perhaps it's not the path to take.

Wellness and forgiveness

Here is another couple of direct questions for you to ponder.

Q: If you have been hurt or harmed or wronged in any way, what are your options?
Q: If you have hurt or harmed or wronged someone else in any way, what are your options?

Might there be a choice to make between doing something about it and doing nothing? Might there be a decision to make as to whether you can move on from the pain/shame or whether you cannot? Which then might raise the question: Can I truly move on without some form of letting go, without some form of forgiveness, either to another or to myself (or both)?

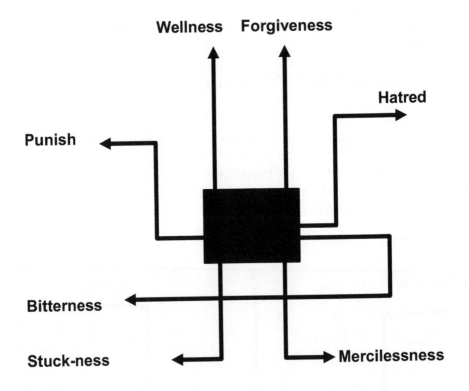

Forgiveness

In Polynesian culture, particularly in Hawaii, forgiveness and reconciliation are an important part of avoiding sickness. They have a word, *Ho'o pono pono*, which translates into English as: "To put to rights." They also have the following mantra:

"I'M SORRY. PLEASE FORGIVE ME. THANK YOU. I LOVE YOU."

Q: How much does guilt, shame and/or blame affect your life?

A:

Q: How much does anger, frustration, hatred and/or bitterness towards others affect your life?

A:

Q: Would you benefit from being able to let go of certain thoughts and feelings and to receive forgiveness from yourself?

A:

Q: Would you benefit from being able to let go of certain thoughts and feelings that are aimed at other people?

A:

Forgiveness Island

Imagine a small island you can go to, by boat, that is set up to help you forgive yourself and/or to forgive others and to allow you to move on in your life. What might this island look like? On the island, you can get to do all sorts of things, but the main focus of the location is to help you to:

- Resolve internal and external conflicts.
- Find ways of existing other than to punish/hate yourself and others.
- Explore the length and breadth of forgiveness and self-forgiveness.
- Let go of your shame, guilt and blame.
- Release your anger.
- Leave aspects of yourself behind on the island that you do not want to take home with you.
- Heal wounds and move forward in your life.

We are soon going to encourage you to create your own forgiveness island, one that you can then walk around, explore and engage in – on an imaginary level. For the time being, however, we will give you a description of the Self Detective forgiveness island, which you may also wish to experience.

The Self Detective forgiveness island

The first thing you notice as you step from your boat onto the beach of Forgiveness Island is how quiet and peaceful it is. Apart from the odd sound of a bird, the lapping of the sea and a light breeze in your ear, the place feels exceptionally peaceful.

The next thing you notice as you make your way up a sandy path is a huge waving flag with the words of the Ho'o Pono Pono mantra on it: "I'm sorry. Please forgive me. Thank you. I love you."

Once you reach the top of the path, the sand gives way to grass and flowers. The ground is flat and even beneath your feet. You have a choice of paths. You walk to the left and follow a border of purple hyacinths – a flower that symbolises forgiveness.

You briefly enter a small woodland. The trees are covered with messages that other people have written either by laboriously cutting out letter shapes on the leaves or else by writing on a label and tying it to a branch. You read what they say. You then notice a pile of pens and labels on the ground. You pick one up and write a message that you attach to a tree.

Further along you come to a wishing well. You close your eyes, throw a coin down the well and when you hear a splash you make a wish.

Past the wishing well there are two signs pointing in opposite directions, one says *Animals* the other says *Humans*. If you follow the animal sign you will get to spend time in a sanctuary for small creatures. Instead you follow the other sign which takes you into a field full of random pieces of wood, nails and hammers, alongside thirty or so people. Nobody says a word, but they smile at you as pass them and you nod your head as you look at the structures that they are making to express what forgiveness means to them.

You reach a river. It is called Mercy. Looking down on the water from a bridge, you take from your backpack a paper boat you made for this very occasion. You drop the boat into the river and watch it float out to sea. You hadn't planned to wade into the water, but the urge is strong, so you take off your shoes and socks, roll up your trousers and immerse yourself in the coolness and the strength of the river Mercy.

On the other side of the bridge is an area of giant-sized mirrors that reflect the beauty of the surrounding nature. You are encouraged to sit on a stone and view yourself as part of the environment. After a spell, you do feel strangely connected to the landscape.

You are almost ready to leave the island. There is but one last thing to do. You get out your map of the island and look to find where the burial ground is sited. (Here you will find a patch of land, two feet square, that has been reserved for you.) When you get there, you find hundreds of rows of coloured stones, marking out each person's plot.

You get out a hand trowel and start to dig. Once you have created a hole big enough, you place the items you have brought with you into the hole and cover it with soil. You then pick a stone from a central barrel, place it on your allotment and take a picture of it.

As you return to your boat on the beach, you inhale the air and notice how much lighter you feel. You rub your shoulders and realise that the tension has been lifted. You are no longer holding any grudge. You have walked away from the past and you are now looking forward to returning home, without the hurt and pain you came with.

My Forgiveness Island

You are now invited to draw (or write or describe aloud) your own forgiveness island.

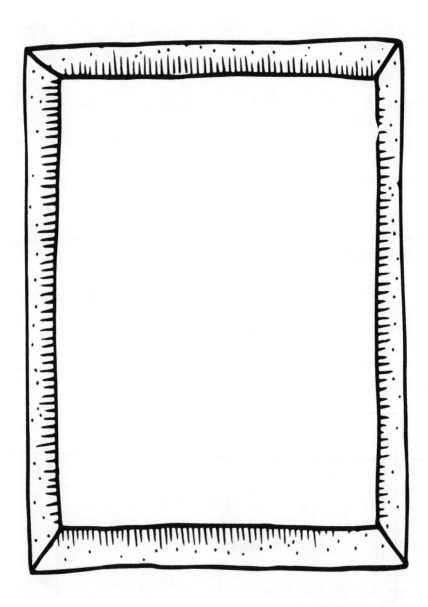

PART 7.

Recognising when you have limited options

 Sometimes we can put ourselves under a lot of pressure to do something that will improve the quality of our lives, by trying to resolve a dilemma or a problem. But what if we can't change or alter our situation? What if we are blocked or restricted in our options or our movement? Surely in these cases it is better to recognise that we cannot do very much, rather than invest time and effort for little reward and plenty of frustration and upset?

Another way of phrasing this is to ask, "when is it better for you to let go of **hope** than it is to keep hold of it?"

Below are some examples of when we have little wiggle room.

Double-bind

Being in a double-bind situation can be really tough and destructive, because whatever you do will be wrong, since you are in a no-win position. It could be that you are given two instructions that conflict or contradict one other. It could be that you are going to be told off no matter what you do.

Sometimes, whether consciously or unconsciously, people use double-binds to control others: to confuse them and manipulate them. Often the most damaging time to have to deal with a double-bind is as a child, when your parents give you an impossible mixed message:

They may say, "Come and give me a kiss." Yet, when you go to give them a kiss, they pull away from you.
They may say, "If you love me you will do as I say."
They may say, "You have to go to the toilet now" (when you do not need to go).

Gregory Bateson, an anthropologist, looked into this and saw that being trapped in a double-bind environment can lead to schizophrenia – that is to say, confusions and distortions in the way we think and communicate.

Damned if you do	Damned if you don't

Yet there is a way out of a double-bind.
It comes when you stop seeing it as a big deal.
It comes when you stop buying into the reality of other people. It comes when you remove other people's goal posts and start to move through life using your own set of rules, your own internal compass and your own codes.

A square peg in a round hole

If you are a square peg in a round hole, it means you will never fit into the hole, no matter what you do (unless you are able to bend your shape and become something that is no longer you). Accepting that you do not fit into a social gathering may save you a lot of trouble. However, if you have to fit in, because there is no other choice, then maybe it is important to be aware of who you really are and where you started from, so you can go back to being you when the environment is less hostile.

Catch 22

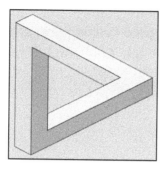

A paradox is a statement that at first sight may appear to make sense but which is actually illogical, incorrect, contradictory or may contain truth and falsehood at the same time.

Catch 22 is a paradox from which you cannot escape, because you are blocked by impractical or unfair rules and regulations.

Joseph Heller published the novel *Catch 22* in 1961. The book is full of crazy paradoxes that highlight the absurdity of war, the military and bureaucracy, as well as abuses of power that hide in plain sight.

Here are some quotes from the text:

> "Catch 22 says they have the right to do anything we can't stop them from doing."

> "From now on I'm thinking only of me."
> Major Danby replied indulgently with a superior smile, "But, Yossarian, suppose everyone felt that way."
> "Then," said Yossarian, "I'd certainly be a damned fool to feel any other way, wouldn't I?"

> "Victory gave us such insane delusions of grandeur that we helped start a world war we hadn't a chance of winning. But now that we are losing again, everything has taken a turn for the better, and we will certainly come out on top again if we succeed in being defeated."

A classic example of a catch 22 is being encouraged to do whatever you want, so long as the powers-that-be agree with it.

[Similarly, **Hobson's Choice** is when you are free to make the choice – even though there is only one choice that is on offer. Another way of setting out the choice is to say 'Take it or leave it' or 'It's my way or the highway.']

Zugzwang

The definition of this German word is a situation where you have to undertake an action that is to your own disadvantage. It is often associated with games, such as chess.

Sometimes we are forced to move, even though we do not want to, as doing so would result in a negative impact on our lives. For example, we are told to move out of a house because the landlord does not want us there anymore, or because a relationship has broken down, yet we do not want to leave.

Deadlock

When no progress can be made between two opposing factions, they can be said to be in deadlock. Other words to describe this situation may be stalemate, standstill or stand-off.

Bound by duty and/or loyalty

Are you obliged to do things out of a sense of duty and loyalty? Are your values unquestionable? For some, it would be unthinkable to put their own needs before others.

For some, their country will always come first. For some, there is no choice in the matter.

Vicious circle

A situation or problem that just gets worse and worse when the elements that create the hostile environment continue to rub up against other, without hope of an end or respite. Or where solving one part of the situation creates a new problem or reactivates the original trouble.

For example: You suffer from chronic pain. You are given some medicine to help to alleviate the pain. The medicine gives you unpleasant side effects. You try another medicine. This seems to work, until its potency weakens. You stop taking the medicine because you are in pain. Now you are left with even more pain than before. So, you try some new medication...

Q: Can you think of times in your own life when you may have encountered some of these situations?

Q: Can you take the time to write down the story of what happened at the beginning, during and how it ended (or how it is likely to end)?

Situation	Start	Middle	Ending
Double-bind			
A square peg in a round hole			
Catch 22			
Zugzwang			
Deadlock			
Bound by duty and/or loyalty			
Vicious circle			

Learned helplessness

If you have suffered pain, hurt or distress on multiple occasions and it seems as though there is no chance of a change or an end in sight, at what point would you abandon all hope and resign yourself to defeat?

Learned helplessness is about giving up, because that is a better option that continuously trying in vain. For some people giving up can lead to symptoms of long-term depression, while for other people it is seen as a positive, since they can now focus on other aspects of their life where they can realistically hope for change.

The American psychologist Martin Seligman conducted a number of questionable experiments on dogs in the late 1960s. Using different groupings of dogs and electric shocks, he found that the dogs who had a history of being shocked and who had been led to believe that nothing they did could stop the discharge of electricity, lay down and gave up, whereas the groups of dogs that did not have such a history, found it within themselves to escape the shocks.

If you had been continuously rejected for positions of employment, at what point might you give up looking for work?

If you were kidnapped, on what day might you give up hope of ever being freed?

If you are in an abusive relationship, at what point might you decide to stop hoping that things will improve?

Q: Can you give some examples in your life where you gave up or resigned yourself to defeat? What happened next?

Stoicism

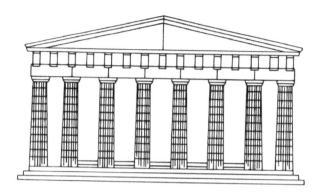

The school of philosophy that started in ancient Greece has many aspects to it. The ones that we are most interested in are the wise nuggets that can help us to move on in life, instead of getting bogged down by negativity and despair.

Below are some pointers as to how being stoic can help us cope better in life.

A stoic person:

- Is calm when under pressure
- Knows when to fight their battles
- Deals with the world as it is, rather than what it could be
- Needs very little for a content life
- Delights in the smaller details in life: the fact that they have a roof over their head, some food in their belly, that they are watered, that they have clean clothes
- Takes responsibility for their own life
- Strives for self-improvement and self-control
- Lives every day as though it is their last
- Acts rather than ponders; acts rather than being helpless
- Eats to live rather than lives to eat
- Embraces failure as an experience
- Rejects vanity and pride

"If you want any good, get it from within."
"It's not what happens to you, but how you react to it that matters."
"Happiness and freedom begin with a clear understanding of one principle: some things are within your control and some things are not."
Epictetus

"There are two ways to get enough.
One is to continue to accumulate more and more.
The other is to desire less."
Gilbert Keith Chesterton

"Recovery is my best revenge."
Carolyn Spring

"Expectation is the root of all heartache."
William Shakespeare

A stoic person recognises that there is no point in getting frustrated with themselves or with the outside world. Nor is there anything to gain from grumbling or complaining. They know that people are doing the best that they can and if their best isn't really good enough, then so be it: let it go.

We have shortened this to:

"Don't get mizzy, get bizzy."

PART 8.

Defence mechanisms
(Developed by Sigmund Freud and Anna Freud)

Protecting our 'self' from perceived threats by using all sorts of ingenious psychological methods is something that we all do at different moments in our life. Often, we do not know we are using defence mechanisms at the time – which just goes to show how devious and how instinctive these functions of our brain can be.

Why is it worth knowing about them?

As with all things related to our psychological make-up, a greater understanding of the mind can lead us to greater choices in life, which in turn can improve our overall well-being.

As you will see from reading on, there are a heck of a lot of ways in which our minds can change, distort or warp reality. Some of these ways are quite straightforward and easy to explain, while others take a bit longer to understand.

Forgetting (repression)

If an event or a time in your life is painful, one of the easiest ways to deal with it is to forget that it ever happened. We can do this simply by pushing it into the furthest reaches of our mind/body/soul.

While this may be a very important method of coping at the time, in years to come it may be difficult to keep the lid on it, as pain has a habit of rising to the surface and spilling out.

It didn't happen (denial)

If 'it' (whatever it may be) didn't happen, then there is no need to be distressed about it... except that 'it' will become harder and harder to deny when it starts popping into your head with greater frequency and begins to wear you down.

It wasn't me – it was you (projection)

Here is a great opportunity to blame someone else for what happened, or to put all the dislike about yourself onto someone else, because the truth is too upsetting. Sometimes what you hate about someone is the very thing you don't like about yourself.

I can't express how I feel to the person I want to, so I'll take it out on someone else instead (displacement)

This is about dumping or off-loading on people (or pets) (or objects) who have nothing to do with the cause of your upset/pain/anger, etc.

Making unacceptable behaviour acceptable (sublimation)

If I can channel my dark side into something that is judged to be okay by my partner/friends/family/ community/society, then I can maintain my status as well as my relationships (as opposed to ending up in prison or being isolated/alienated) e.g. boxing, gaming, writing horror stories, acting, performing, etc.

Mimicking aspects of others (introjection)

This is the opposite of 'it wasn't me – it was you.'
In times of distress or threat to yourself, it might be the best option to behave like someone else, e.g. if I shape my hair to look like Ingrid Bergman, I will have all the confidence and sassiness that she has.

Removing the emotion from a memory (isolation)

This allows you think about an otherwise painful or upsetting episode without feeling it, just as though you were merely reporting the events.

Going back in time (regression)

If the pressure to be a certain age is too much for you, going back to a younger age might help reduce the stress. (Think of the times when you might have curled up in a foetal position at night.)

Day-dreaming (fantasising)

Having fantasies, especially about the things that 'could have been' in your life, are a way of dealing with disappointments, or of ending things that didn't have an ending. This is a great way to re-write your history.

Going into your head rather than your heart (intellectualising)

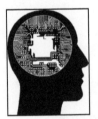

If you are hurting, you might want to think away what is causing the pain by giving yourself a rational explanation: e.g. "I failed because I didn't want to pass the stupid test anyway."

Going over the top in order to avoid feelings of inferiority (compensating)

You may have lost out on one particular thing, but you can always remind yourself of plenty of times when you did plenty of really good things: when you were at the very top of your game.

Doing or saying the exact opposite of what you want to do or say (reaction formation)

If you can't say how awful you think the dress is, you might end up going to the opposite extreme of being extremely complimentary about it. If you have a strong desire, which you cannot accept of yourself, you might not only deny it but also make a point of doing something that suggests your desires lie in other areas.

Because I've been horrible I will now be super-nice (undoing)

If you have just shouted at someone at dinner time and you have reduced them to tears, you might make a show of moving away from that 'horrible' side of you by tidying the table or doing the washing, which is the nicer side to you.

After-thought

If you are aware of participating in any of these defence mechanisms and you are struggling with the consequences, it might be time to address your issues and take a different course of action.

PART 9.

Coping planner

In this section, we will be looking at different ways to:

- Start up a new coping strategy
- Start up a new routine
- Change from one coping strategy to another one
- Focus on your emotional and problem-solving needs
- Look at ways to manage a relapse
- Work out when, where, what and with whom makes you stressed, anxious and/or depressed
- Work out when, where, how, with what and with whom makes you unstressed, less anxious and less depressed.

We will also be bringing everything together from each of the previous sections so that you can, if you wish, begin to formulate a wide-ranging plan of action.

My coping questions

Q: What are the 8 most likely coping methods that I will use?
1.
2.
3.
4.
5.
6.
7.
8.

Q: What are my 3 most effective coping strategies?
1.
2.
3.

Q: What are my 3 least effective coping strategies?
1.
2.
3.

Q: What are my 3 most healthy coping strategies?
1.
2.
3.

Q: What are my 3 least healthy coping strategies?
1.
2.
3.

Q: Which people are good for me when I am up against it?

A:

Q: What/who do I need to avoid when I am up against it?

A:

Q: What situations, events or environments stress me out the most?

A:

Q: When/where/with whom/what do I most need to use a coping method for?

A:

Q: What adjustments could I make to my life to help me cope better?

A:

Q: What things will help me when I need to solve a problem?

A:

Q: What things help me when I need to manage my emotions?

A:

Q: What do I tend to do when I get stressed?

A:

Q: What are the tell-tale signs that I am stressing?

A:

Q: What triggers my stress?

A:

Introducing a new coping method into our lives

Let us now focus our minds on how we can introduce a new coping strategy into our lives. For, while it may seem like a simple task, without the motivation and determination to keep it in mind/fit it into our routine/stick it in our to-do list, it is going to get forgotten about.

One way to remember the new coping strategy (CS) is to set about launching it. Have a date when you will use it or practise it. Give yourself a week's run-up to the time and date.
E.g.:

Name of CS:
Brief description:
Starting date:
Time:
Length of time:

Once the time has come and gone, you may wish also to rate how effective the CS was and whether or not any tweaks or adaptations need to be made.

Rating:
Modifications:

Secondly, keep the strategy in mind by either putting the name or a drawing of it in your diary. You could put up a chart on the wall, or carry something around with you that will remind you what you are doing, such as wearing a wristband.

Thirdly, do you need to do anything in preparation of the CS, such as buying an item of clothing or rearranging your ongoing daily commitment?

New coping strategies case study: Leslie's realistic approach

Leslie likes the idea of so many coping strategies, yet she is also a realist and knows that when it comes down to it, she doesn't have a lot of time or motivation in his life right now to fit many of them in. She decides to design a recovery bag over the course of the week, to do one short session of physical exercise a week, to eat one new piece of fruit/veg a week and to focus on a mantra that she can learn to repeat in hher head over and over again.

Leslie wrote each one down like this one:

Coping strategy #1: Mantra	Details:
When	In the morning when I wake up. To and from work. Before I go to sleep.
Where	In bed. On the bus.
How	By repeating the same words over and over in my head for at least 3 minutes at a time.
With what	With my own personal mantra.
With whom	With myself.

You are encouraged to do the same, using the same template, below.

My new coping strategies details

Coping strategy #1:	Details:
When	
Where	
How	
With what	
With whom	

Coping strategy #2:	Details:
When	
Where	
How	
With what	
With whom	

Coping strategy #3:	Details:
When	
Where	
How	
With what	
With whom	

Coping strategy #4:	Details:
When	
Where	
How	
With what	
With whom	

Example of a weekly coping activity planner

There is a real difference between thinking you will do something and actively planning for something – and then being held accountable to that plan by recording your results.

Coping activity	Day 1	Day 2	Day 3	Day 4	Day 5	Day 6	Day 7
Porridge in the morning	✓	✓	✓	✓	✓	✓	✓
Half an hour exercise	✓	✓	✓	✓	✓		✓
One hour exercise	✓		✓		✓		
Abstinence from alcohol	✓	✓		✓	✓	✓	
Communicate with a new person	✓	✓	✓	✓	✓		
Ten minutes of calm	✓	✓	✓	✓	✓	✓	
Computer off before 10pm	✓	✓			✓	✓	

You will notice that this particular person has managed to do a lot of the activities that they set themselves, and rather than be dismayed by the times they didn't get to achieve their aim, they are happy with their progress.

My weekly coping activity planner

Coping activity	Day 1	Day 2	Day 3	Day 4	Day 5	Day 6	Day 7

Replacing an old coping strategy with a new one

If a coping strategy is no longer as effective as it once was or if you now recognise that it isn't healthy for you to continue with it, you may wish to find an alternative – something that is going to do the same job or a better job. As a straightforward exercise can you think of any possible replacements to any of your existing CSs?

Existing strategy #1:	
Alternative strategy:	

Existing strategy #2:	
Alternative strategy:	

Existing strategy #3:	
Alternative strategy:	

Sometimes it can be relatively easy to swap one CS for another: you can simply plan for the swap-over date and away you go.

Name and description of old CS:
Name and description of new CS:
How will the change will take place?
Starting date of swap:

At other times you might need to give it some thought, especially if you have been using the old CS for quite a while. It is likely that a part of you will want to resist this change in some way – the part of you that perhaps doesn't like change, or the part that has become addicted, or compelled, to keep the old CS going. In which case, it may be important to recognise this fact and find ways to avoid an internal conflict by:

(i) writing down or speaking aloud all the benefits that will go with making the change, as well as being realistic about what you will lose.

Benefits and positive consequences to changing	Drawbacks and negative consequences to changing

(ii) Introduce the new CS slowly, while also steadily withdrawing from the old one. This is known as **tapering** or a **step-by-step approach** or a **cross-fade.**

New CS

Old CS

This approach, if appropriate, could be planned as below:

Day 1	Day 2	Day 3	Day 4	Day 5	Day 6	Day 7
New CS	Old CS	New CS	Old CS	New CS	Old CS	New CS

Day 8	Day 9	Day 10	Day 11	Day 12	Day 13	Day 14
New CS	Old CS	New CS	New CS	Old CS	New CS	New CS

Day 15	Day 16	Day 17	Day 18	Day 19	Day 20	Day 21
New CS	Old CS	New CS	New CS	New CS	New CS	New CS

Or like this: with a slow transition of time donated from the old CS to the new CS.

	Day 1 (mins)	Day 2 (mins)	Day 3 (mins)	Day 4 (mins)	Day 5 (mins)
Old CS					
New CS					

	Day 6 (mins)	Day 7 (mins)	Day 8 (mins)	Day 9 (mins)	Day 10 (mins)
Old CS					
New CS					

Relapses and losing routines

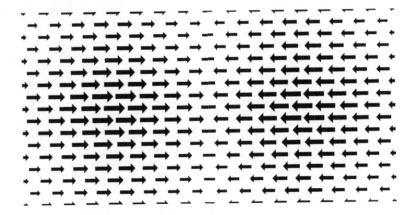

It's to be anticipated that some people will have relapses from time to time. This often happens at the early stages of abstinence, or introducing a coping strategy, or making a transition from one strategy to another.

There is a fine line between not beating yourself up about relapsing and being motivated enough about your well-being to be concerned by a lapse.

Knowing how devious, cunning and self-sabotaging our minds can be, just reading the information above will be enough for some crafty souls to think that they now have permission to fail or relapse whenever they want to.

So perhaps one of the secrets of maintaining coping strategies is to get to know yourself (and all the various parts of yourself), especially your destructive side, or the side that is willing to compromise your wellness for the sake of a short-term reward/fix.

Below is a classic internal monologue when it comes to abstinence:

"You are doing so well giving up cigarettes, I think you deserve a treat. How about a couple of puffs on a cigarette?"

Below are some pointers to consider when you relapse or when you break a routine:

- You know yourself better than anyone else: so how big a deal is it?
- Can you learn from what happened?
- Can you still continue on your way, or do you need to start again from day one?
- Do you need a mantra or an affirmation to help you with your set-back?
- If you are relapsing regularly, how best can you manage this situation?
- Realistically, what steps do you need to take now?
- Are you still being fair/kind to yourself?
- If you have slipped out of a routine, can you set up a new planner to get you back on track?

If you recognise that you are not coping and that you are unwell, perhaps you need to consider the following options:

- Seek help from friends or family
- Seek help professionally
- Seek help from a crisis team
- Devote yourself to recovery

GOOD LUCK WITH WHICHEVER DIRECTION YOU TAKE

PART 10.

Pulling things together from "Coping Strategies" section

SD Skills I have used in this section:

SD Skills I would like to develop:

SD Tools I have used in this section

SD Tools I would like to develop further:

My updated SD case file now concerns:

My (revised) framework for SD is:

My SD discoveries so far are:

My (revised) SD goals are:

My next move is:

PART 11

MY ROUGH NOTES & IDEAS

MY ROUGH NOTES & IDEAS

MY ROUGH NOTES & IDEAS

MY ROUGH DRAWINGS & DOODLES

MY ROUGH DRAWINGS & DOODLES

Lightning Source UK Ltd.
Milton Keynes UK
UKHW010635200121
377380UK00001B/119